Usborne
Big Picture Book
GENERAL KNOWLEDGE

James Maclaine

ILLUSTRATED BY
Annie Carbo

DESIGNED BY
Nancy Leschnikoff, Helen Edmonds
& Emily Barden

CONTENTS

AROUND THE WORLD

There are over **7.4 BILLION** people living in almost **200** countries around the world.

The world has seven continents and five oceans. Their names are on this map in CAPITAL letters. The numbers on the map show the places also mentioned in the facts.

The five smallest countries would all fit inside Walt Disney World, Florida.

1 VATICAN CITY

2 MONACO

3 NAURU

4 TUVALU

5 SAN MARINO

6 Canada has the longest coastline. It's over 200,000km (124,000 miles) long.

More than 88% of all the people in the world live in its northern half.

NORTH AMERICA

PACIFIC OCEAN

ATLANTIC OCEAN

SOUTH AMERICA

7 More billionaires live in New York than any other city.

More than **885,000KM** (**550,000 MILES**) of undersea cables connect people using the internet around the world.

On June 20, 1970, Dave Kunst set off on a walk around the world. He completed his journey on October 5, 1974.

8 A third of the world's coffee is produced in Brazil.

9 La Rinconada, in Peru, is the highest town in the world. It's in the Andes Mountains and **5,100M (16,700FT)** above sea level.

10 Águila Islet is the southernmost point of South America.

In a comparison of average heights around the world, men from Holland and women from Latvia are tallest.

Men from East Timor and women from Guatemala are shortest.

20 19 18 17

16

People have lived in Aleppo, Syria, for around 8,000 years. No other city has been inhabited longer.

ARCTIC OCEAN

EUROPE

19
20 5
2
1
16

ASIA

15

China shares a border with more countries than any other – 14 in total.

Nepal · Pakistan · Afghanistan · Tajikistan · Kyrgyzstan · Kazakhstan · India · Mongolia · Russia · North Korea · Vietnam · Laos · Myanmar · Bhutan

14 12
13

AFRICA

INDIAN OCEAN

11

3
4

18

AUSTRALASIA

There are twice as many kangaroos as people in Australia.

SOUTHERN OCEAN

ANTARCTICA

12

The flag of Bangladesh has a red circle slightly to the left of its middle. This is so the circle looks central when the flag is flying.

11

Lesotho is a type of country called an 'enclave'. It's surrounded by just one other country – South Africa.

13

The capital city of Thailand is Bangkok. Its full name in Thai is a whopping **169** letters long.

14 The Kumbh Mela festival attracts the biggest crowds of any festival. Over **30 MILLION** people attended the event in Allahabad, India, on one day in 2013.

Bangkok's name in full: Krungthepmahanakhon Amonrattanakosin Mahintharayutthaya Mahadilokphop Noppharatratchathaniburirom Udomratchaniwetmahasathan Amonphimanawatansathit Sakkathattiyawitsanukamprasit

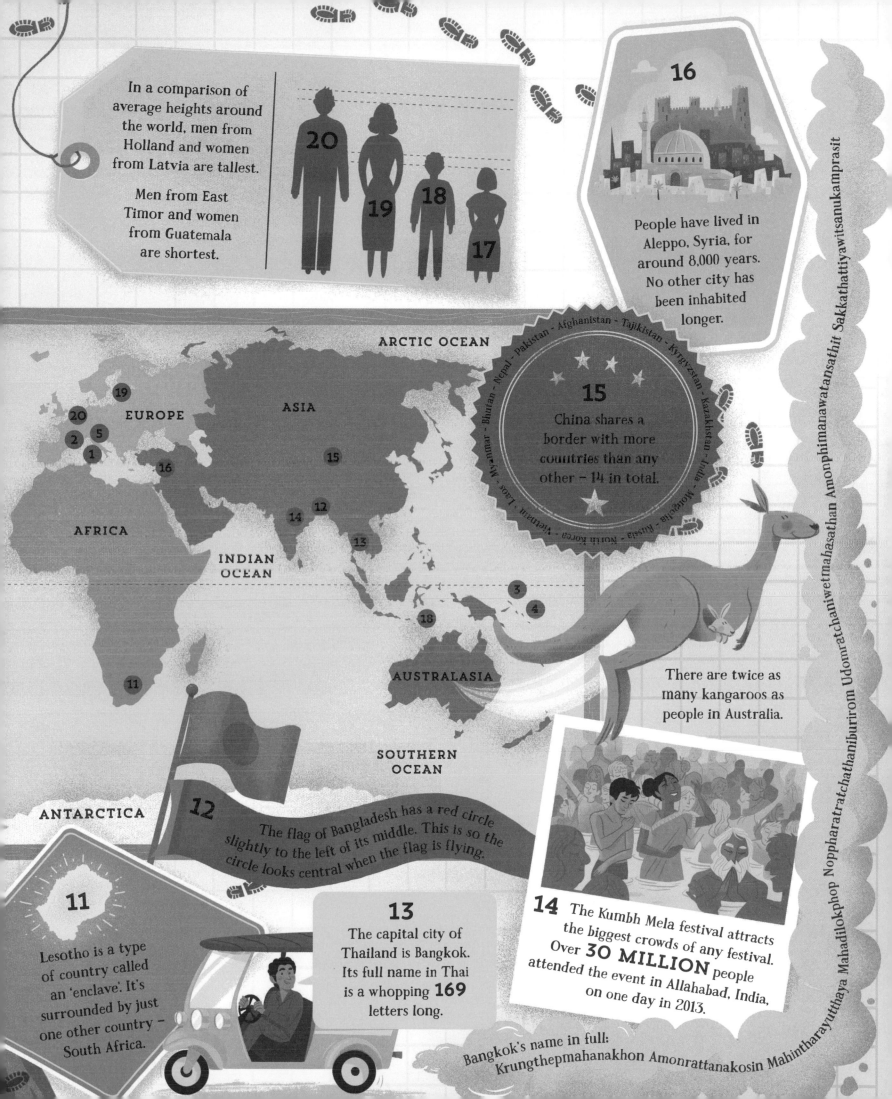

ANIMALS

The insect with the widest wingspan is the white witch moth.

There are more than **20 BILLION** chickens in the world. That's around three chickens for every person.

If all the animals in the world had a running race, the twelve fastest would finish in this order...

JOINT **6**TH
BLACKBUCK & HARE

10TH PLACE
KANGAROO

9TH
AFRICAN WILD DOG

8TH
JACKRABBIT

7TH
GREYHOUND

The first type of dog to win Best in Show at Crufts – a dog show in England – was a greyhound in 1928.

Giant tortoises can live for more than 150 years.

A baby kangaroo, or joey, stays in its mother's pouch until it's eight months old.

Dwarf geckos are the smallest lizards in the world.

Actual size

A single millipede can have as many as **750** legs, although its name actually means 'a thousand feet'.

The strongest insects are dung beetles.

They can drag balls of dung 1,000 times heavier than themselves.

Alpine swifts can fly for more than 200 days without stopping.

Sword-billed hummingbirds have beaks that can be longer than their bodies.

I eat almost nothing except bamboo, but occasionally I eat a rat.

Giant panda

FINISH

JOINT **5**TH
WILDEBEEST & LION

2ND
OSTRICH

Ostriches are the largest birds.

1ST
CHEETAH

4TH
SPRINGBOK

3RD
PRONGHORN

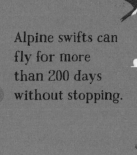

All wild cats live alone, except for lions. They live in groups called prides.

The suckers on an octopus's eight arms help it to taste things.

Sea lions can walk on land using their flippers...

...but seals have to shuffle along on their tummies.

Millions of herring swim together in the largest groups of any fish.

An octopus can change the look of its skin so it can blend in with the ocean floor.

A pufferfish swallows lots of water to puff its body into a large ball.

This stops other fish from eating it.

Lobsters have blue blood.

YOUR BODY

INCHES
CM

1
2
3
4
5
6
7
8
9
10
11
12
13
14
15

If you didn't have your hair cut, it could grow around 15cm (6in) in a year.

You are born with **270** bones inside your body, but some join together as you grow. When you're an adult, you'll have **206** bones.

(The scientific names of some of your bones are shown underneath.)

SKULL (CRANIUM)

JAWBONE (MANDIBLE)

COLLARBONE (CLAVICLE)

BREASTBONE (STERNUM)

You have **12** pairs of ribs.

UPPER ARM BONE (HUMERUS)

LOWER ARM BONES (RADIUS AND ULNA)

There are **33** round bones called vertebrae in your spine.

PELVIS

THIGH BONE (FEMUR) – your biggest bone

KNEECAP (PATELLA)

Almost half the bones in your body are in your hands and feet.

CALF BONE (FIBULA)

SHIN BONE (TIBIA)

Your blood is made in your bones.

BRAIN
Your brain keeps growing until you're around 25 years old.

You blink around 15 times a minute.

It takes 15 years to grow your 32 adult teeth, starting when you're around age six.

Your smallest bone is the stapes inside each ear. It's this size:

You use more muscles in your face to smile than to frown.

Can you feel a dip at the base of your throat? It's called the 'suprasternal notch'.

You shed tiny flakes of dead skin every day. They make up most of the dust in your home.

Your skin is your largest organ.

The shortest adult ever was Chandra Bahadur Dangi from Nepal. He was 54.6cm (1ft, 9in) tall.

At 2.72m (8ft, 11in) tall, Robert Wadlow from the US was the tallest person ever.

The medical term for freckles is 'ephelides'.

Everyone has their own unique pattern of fingerprints.

Your toe and fingernails grow faster in warm weather.

Most people's lower arms are the same length as their feet.

A muscle in your shoulder is known as the 'deltoid' muscle because it's triangle-shaped like the Greek letter delta: Δ.

Your longest muscles connect your hips and knees. They are called 'sartorius muscles'.

About **70%** of your body is water.

When your kidneys are fully grown, they're the size of a computer mouse.

LEFT LUNG

You use your lungs to take up to 1,200 breaths every hour.

HEART

There are 78 organs in the human body.

Your heart beats around **100,000** times a day.

RIGHT LUNG

Your right lung is bigger than your left lung.

STOMACH

Your stomach makes acid that's strong enough to dissolve some metals.

LEFT KIDNEY

LIVER

– your heaviest organ

RIGHT KIDNEY

LARGE INTESTINE

SMALL INTESTINE

Your small intestine is **6M (20FT)** long – four times longer than your large intestine.

ON THE MOVE

The blades of Russian helicopters rotate clockwise, but American ones rotate in the opposite direction.

The first red London bus was introduced in 1907.

The oldest steam train still running today is The Fairy Queen in India. It was built in 1855.

Bikes called 'tandems' have more than one rider.

Mining trucks have bigger wheels than any other vehicles. They're almost as tall as I am.

The longest bicycle ever made is over three times longer than a bus.

At least one in every five cars in the world is white.

The Channel Tunnel between England and France is the longest undersea tunnel.

The Beijing Subway system is the busiest in the world. Over **9 MILLION** people use it every day.

The part of a hot-air balloon that fills with air is called the envelope.

At any moment there can be more than **7,000** aircraft flying in the sky.

The first motorcycles and cars were invented more than 130 years ago.

The back of a boat is called the stern...

Boats with sails have been used for more than 5,000 years.

...and the front is the bow.

The Italian city Venice has 177 canals instead of roads, so even its fire engines are boats.

...the bottom is the keel...

343M **(1,125**FT**) TALL**

The tallest bridge in the world is the Millau Viaduct in France.

On most of the world's roads, drivers have to drive on the right.

A gondola is a type of boat used in Venice.

It's rowed with a long oar.

Submarines extract oxygen from sea water, so the crew inside can breathe.

It took **61 DAYS** for the first submarine to travel around the world underwater in 1960. Its name was USS *Triton*.

9

FOOD AND DRINK

Tomatoes can be green, yellow, purple or black, as well as red.

The heaviest cabbage ever grown weighed more than **60KG (132LBS)**...

...or **240** packs or sticks of butter.

At the annual La Tomatina festival in Spain, people throw around **1 MILLION** tomatoes at each other.

The most widely eaten meat in the world is pork.

Dark soy sauce is less salty than light soy sauce.

It takes someone **50** licks on average to eat a scoop of ice cream.

Ketchup was made from pickled fish, mushrooms or walnuts before tomatoes were used instead.

Watermelon is more than **90%** water.

The study of fruit is called 'pomology'.

Cakes turn hard when they're stale...

...but cookies and crackers turn soft.

The tea bag was invented in 1901.

Crushed garlic tastes stronger than chopped garlic.

X 40

=

Around 40 olives are pressed to make just one tablespoon of olive oil.

Approximately **40%** of all 'sandwiches' sold are burgers.

When milk turns sour it separates into...

...curds that are solid...

...and a liquid called whey.

Curds are used to make cheese.

Both salt and pepper have been used as money in different parts of the world.

There are more than **450** baked beans in a standard can.

Apples and raw onions taste very similar if you eat them while pinching your nose.

People opened cans with a hammer and chisel before the can opener was invented in 1855.

The prongs of a fork are called tines.

TOP 5 MOST EATEN FOODS AROUND THE WORLD:

1. **MAIZE (CORN)**

2. **RICE**

3. **WHEAT**
Wheat is ground into flour to make bread or pasta for example.

4. **POTATOES**

5. **CASSAVA**
The roots of cassava plants can be made into flour or eaten when cooked.

In 1937, Joseph Friedman invented the first bendable straws, so his daughter could drink milkshakes more easily.

The spicy heat of chilies is measured on the Scoville scale.

The hottest chili pepper, the Carolina Reaper, can be more than **1,500,000** Scovilles.

Jalapeño peppers are more than **2,000** Scovilles.

The mildest peppers are **O** Scovilles.

11

NATURAL WONDERS

The strongest gust of wind ever measured blew at a speed of 408km/h (253.5mph) on Barrow Island, in Australia, in 1996.

Jungles cover **2%** of the Earth's surface but they're home to more than **50%** of all known living things.

From its source to the sea, the Danube flows through ten countries – more than any other river.

Geologists have no rules for distinguishing hills from mountains.

There are around **1,500** active volcanoes worldwide.

GERMANY

AUSTRIA

SLOVAKIA

CROATIA

HUNGARY

Around 400,000 types of plants produce flowers. That's around **80%** of all the world's plants.

SERBIA

ROMANIA

BULGARIA

MOLDOVA

UKRAINE

A wave reaches its highest point at its 'crest', then plummets to its lowest point, or 'trough'.

If an earthquake happens under the sea, it can cause towering waves to form. This is called a 'tsunami'.

At more than **1.6KM (1 MILE)** deep, Lake Baikal, in Russia, is the world's deepest lake.

It's home to types of seals and fish that live nowhere else in the world.

Seawater is **3.5%** salt on average.

Corals look like beautiful rocks and plants but they're actually made up of tiny living creatures called polyps.

Different clouds form in the sky depending on how cold and how high up they are. They have different names:

CIRRUS

ALTOCUMULUS

CUMULONIMBUS

The **188** highest mountains in the world are all in Asia.

A baobab tree can store up to **400,000** cups of water in its bulging trunk.

A bolt of lightning can be a blistering 30,000°C (54,000°F). That's five times hotter than the surface of the Sun.

More water flows down the Khone Falls, in Laos, than any other waterfall. It could fill four Olympic swimming pools every second.

The largest area of sand in the world is the Rub' al Khali desert in the Arabian Peninsula.

It doesn't have to rain for you to see a rainbow. You can sometimes see one in mist near a waterfall.

A desert is any place where less than **25CM (10IN)** of rain falls each year.

The most powerful whirlpool, or 'maelstrom', in the world is near the coast of Norway.

After the world's five oceans (Pacific, Atlantic, Indian, Southern and Arctic), the largest sea is the Philippine Sea.

This makes icy Antarctica, where it hardly ever rains, the largest desert in the world.

Around **70%** of all the world's fresh water is frozen as ice over Antarctica.

Small icebergs are known as 'bergy bits' or 'growlers'.

SPORTS

Australian rules football teams are made up of **18** players – that's more than any other sport.

The balls used in some of the first games of football were inflated pigs' bladders.

100m sprinters run faster when the weather is hot.

American astronaut Alan Shepard played golf on the Moon in 1971.

There can be between 300 and 500 dimples on a typical golf ball.

Polo matches, played on horseback, are divided into several stages called 'chukkas'.

Stefaan Engels from Belgium ran a marathon every day for an entire year, starting in February 2010.

In a game of baseball in 1977, Glenn Burke and Dusty Baker raised their arms and slapped their hands together inventing the high five.

A horse's height is measured to its 'withers' – a ridge between its shoulders.

An Olympic swimming pool contains enough water to fill **7,575,000** empty drink cans.

There are three forms of fencing each fought with a different sword with a different-looking handle.

Foil

Some pools have underwater speakers to help synchronized swimmers perform in time to music.

Épée   Sabre

A group of cyclists in a road race is known as a 'peloton'.

The oldest international sports trophy is the America's Cup for yacht racing. It was first awarded in 1851.

7 events make up a heptathlon competition.

100m hurdles | High jump | Shot put | 200m race | Long jump | Javelin throw | 800m race

The longest point in a tennis tournament lasted 29 minutes in 1984. Vicki Nelson and Jean Hepner hit the ball over the net **643** times before one of them missed.

When volleyball was first played in 1895, it was called 'mintonette'.

Players in New Zealand's rugby union team, the All Blacks, perform a noisy dance known as the 'haka' before every match.

The best ice skaters can spin around on one foot up to 115 times without stopping.

Olympic gold medals are mostly silver. They're only covered in gold.

Sherman Poppen joined two skis together to invent the first snowboard in 1965.

The World Cup final is the most watched sporting event on TV. Almost **1 BILLION** people saw the final in 2014.

The first ice hockey pucks are thought to have been made from frozen cow dung.

The loudest bang ever recorded was heard when the volcanic island Krakatoa exploded in **1883**.

Wolfgang Amadeus Mozart started composing music in **1761** when he was just five years old.

The first ever piano was made in **1700**.

In **1666**, 80% of London was destroyed in what became known as the Great Fire of London.

BACK IN TIME

When did handheld portable phones first go on sale?

1984

START HERE

TODAY

Each of my fingernails is slightly bigger than this page.

The Statue of Liberty was put up in New York in **1886**.

Edmund Hillary from New Zealand and Tenzing Norgay from Nepal were the first climbers to reach the top of Mount Everest in **1953**.

John D. Rockefeller US oil tycoon

I became the world's first billionaire in **1916**.

Fruit flies on board a V2 rocket were the first animals to travel into space and back in **1947**.

The first pencils were made around the year **1560**.

In **1010**, the world's longest river, the Nile, froze. It hasn't frozen again since.

The first person from Europe to sail to North America was Icelandic explorer Leif Ericson around the year **1000**.

I sometimes took part in gladiator fights

COMMODUS
ROMAN EMPEROR
(180-192)

In the year **690**, Wu Zetian became the only woman ever to be Emperor of China.

Fireworks were first made in China before the year **900**.

YEAR 1

There was no year 0. Years before 1 are counted back from then and have BC ('Before Christ') written after them.

In Greece, a baker named Coroebus won the only event at the first ever Olympic Games in **776BC**. It was a running race.

The last mammoths lived on Wrangel Island in the Arctic Ocean around **2,000BC**.

The Great Sphinx and the Great Pyramid of Giza were built around **2,500BC**. This pyramid was the tallest building in the world for almost 4,000 years.

MUSIC

A woman singing a French song called *Au Clair de la Lune* in 1860 is the oldest-known recording of a human voice.

So many fans of the composer Franz Liszt asked for locks of his hair that he started sending his dog's hair instead.

FRANZ LISZT (1811-1886)

My *Minute Waltz* takes more than a minute and a half to play.

FRYDERYK CHOPIN (1810-1849)

There are **52** white keys...

...and **36** black keys on a piano.

No instrument has more strings than a piano. There are over **200** hidden inside.

More people have a harmonica than any other type of instrument.

No band has sold more records than The Beatles.

Snake charmers in India and Pakistan play a wind instrument called a 'pungi'.

A platinum record is awarded to musicians whose albums sell **1 MILLION** copies in the US.

After a performance by the Spanish opera singer Plácido Domingo in 1991, the audience clapped for 1 hour and 20 minutes.

Trombones used to be known as 'sackbuts'.

A violin can be made up of more than **70** wooden pieces.

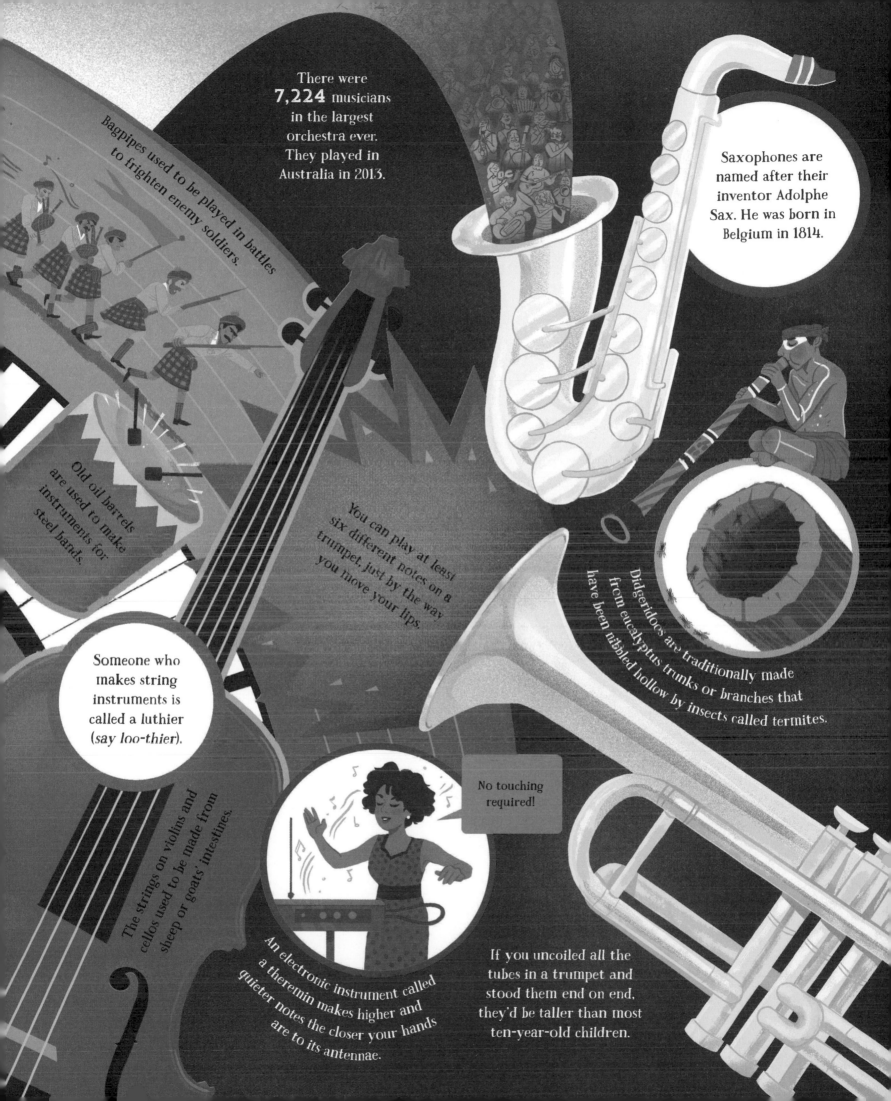

There were **7,224** musicians in the largest orchestra ever. They played in Australia in 2013.

Saxophones are named after their inventor Adolphe Sax. He was born in Belgium in 1814.

Bagpipes used to be played in battles to frighten enemy soldiers.

Old oil barrels are used to make instruments for steel bands.

You can play at least six different notes on a trumpet, just by the way you move your lips.

Didgeridoos are traditionally made from eucalyptus trunks or branches that have been nibbled hollow by insects called termites.

Someone who makes string instruments is called a luthier (*say loo-thier*).

The strings on violins and cellos used to be made from sheep or goats' intestines.

No touching required!

An electronic instrument called a theremin makes higher and quieter notes the closer your hands are to its antennae.

If you uncoiled all the tubes in a trumpet and stood them end on end, they'd be taller than most ten-year-old children.

WHO'S WHO?

The actor with the most nominations for an Oscar statuette is Meryl Streep. She was nominated for the 19th time in 2015.

American chemist Robert Cornelius took the first selfie when he photographed himself in 1839.

The story of the heroic outlaw Robin Hood has been adapted into more than **50** feature films.

Did you know I made around **90** self-portraits?

REMBRANDT VAN RIJN
DUTCH ARTIST
(1606-1669)

Iraqi-British architect Zaha Hadid designed the London Aquatics Centre for the 2012 Olympic Games. She was the first woman to win architecture's highest award, the Pritzker Prize.

Midas of Phrygia was a legendary king who turned everything he touched into gold.

George Washington, the first President of the United States, helped to breed a new type of dog: the American foxhound.

US swimmer Michael Phelps has won **23** Olympic gold medals – more than any other athlete.

German physicist Wilhelm Röntgen gave X-rays their name in 1895.

French chef Auguste Escoffier invented a dessert of peaches, raspberry sauce and vanilla ice cream for Australian soprano Nellie Melba. He called the dish 'Peach Melba'.

Madeleine and Georges de Scudéry wrote *Artamène* – the longest novel ever. It has over **13,000** pages.

At any moment somewhere in the world, actors are performing one of my **37** plays.

No monarch has ruled longer than Sobhuza II who was King of Swaziland for **82** years and **254** days.

The fictional detective Sherlock Holmes took up beekeeping when he retired.

INK

Miguel de Cervantes wrote the best-selling novel of all time: *Don Quixote*. It has sold more than **500 MILLION** copies around the world.

Muhammad Ali became the first boxer to win the world heavyweight title three times.

Nefertiti was an Egyptian queen who lived more than 3,300 years ago. Her name means 'the beautiful woman has arrived'.

St. Valentine is the patron saint of love and beekeepers.

Nero's mother poisoned me with deadly mushrooms.

My name means 'little boots'.

Polish-French scientist Marie Curie studied dangerous radioactive materials. She died over 80 years ago, but her books are still too radioactive to handle.

1ST AUGUSTUS

2ND TIBERIUS

3RD CALIGULA

4TH CLAUDIUS

5TH NERO

THE FIRST FIVE ROMAN EMPERORS

A photo of the Loch Ness Monster, taken in 1934, in fact shows a model head and neck, attached to a toy submarine.

People sometimes mistake lentil-shaped clouds, known as lenticular clouds, for flying saucers.

Vampires really do exist. There are types of bats, finches and moths known as vampires because they eat blood from other animals.

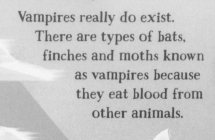

In an Ancient Indian poem called the *Mahabharata*, there's a strange creature known as Navagunjara. It has these body parts:

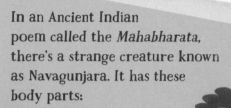

ROOSTER'S HEAD

SNAKE FOR A TAIL

BULL'S HUMP

HUMAN ARM

PEACOCK'S NECK

LEGS OF A DEER, TIGER & ELEPHANT

LION'S BODY

MYTHS AND MONSTERS

Over 500 years ago, an unknown European author wrote the Voynich manuscript in a mysterious language that no one now understands.

According to myth, Greek soldiers hid in a wooden horse to get inside the city of Troy.

I'm a werewolf. In stories, people who turn into wolves or other beasts are said to have the power of 'therianthropy'.

EGYPTIAN GODS AND GODDESSES

The Ancient Egyptians had more than a thousand names for different gods and goddesses. These are just a few of them:

RA
God of the Sun

OSIRIS
God of the underworld

ISIS
Goddess of magic

HATHOR
Goddess of music and love

THOTH
God of wisdom

PTAH
God of craftsmen

People in western North America have carved totem poles for more than 200 years. They're decorated with animals, both mythical and real.

You can tell that I'm a Chinese imperial dragon because I have five claws on each foot. Japanese dragons only have three claws.

I'm a thunderbird. It's said that I cause storms with my wings.

I'm a sea turtle. I represent the world.

Legendary British ruler, King Arthur, is said to have sat with his knights at a round table in his castle, Camelot.

King Arthur's sword, Excalibur, had magical powers that protected him from harm.

Since the 18th century, sailors have told of a ghost ship known as The Flying Dutchman. The ship is fated to sail the seas forever and never reach land.

Strange, flickering light above swamps is known as will-o'-the-wisp, ghost-light or *ignis fatuus* (Latin for 'foolish fire'). It's probably gases burning as things rot, but some people think it's made by fairies.

According to folklore, mandrake plants scream when they're pulled from the ground.

EEEEEE! Our roots look like bodies with heads, arms and legs.

23

This is a pyramidion – a carved stone placed at the very top of a pyramid.

Captain William Kidd is one of the only pirates known to have buried treasure. He hid gold, silver and jewels on Gardiners Island, near New York, in 1699.

Silk is a luxurious material made from silk moth caterpillars. They're fed on white mulberry tree leaves before their cocoons are boiled to make silk threads.

TREASURES

The word for silk farming is 'sericulture' and a silk farm is called a 'magnanery'.

Kimono means a 'thing to wear' in Japanese. It's a fancy type of robe with wide sleeves.

Queen Elizabeth I of England passed a law that forbade anyone but members of the royal family from wearing purple.

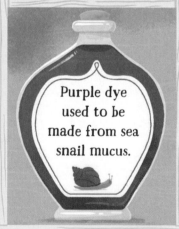
Purple dye used to be made from sea snail mucus.

There are four types of precious gemstones:

DIAMOND **RUBY** **SAPPHIRE** **EMERALD**

All other gemstones are semi-precious, such as...

MALACHITE **OBSIDIAN** **TURQUOISE**

CARNELIAN

The hardness of gemstones is measured on the Mohs scale.

JASPER **AMETHYST** **TOURMALINE**

LAPIS LAZULI **JET**

Porcelain dishes and vases were first made in China around 2,000 years ago.

Lapis lazuli used to be ground into a paint called ultramarine. Ultramarine means 'beyond the sea', because it was imported from Asia into Europe by boat.

Jet is made of wood, from trees similar to the Monkey Puzzle, that has rotted for millions of years.

The things I've seen!

Did you know that most Ancient Greek and Roman marble statues were originally painted?

Aztec rulers wore headdresses made of bright feathers.

Green feathers from a type of bird called the quetzal were the most prized.

The Bank of England keeps million pound notes in its vaults. They're nicknamed 'giants'.

The dollar sign was first used around 240 years ago for the Spanish dollar, or *peso*. First, peso was shortened to Pˢ. Then, the S was written over the P instead: $. This in turn became the symbol we know today.

Collecting stamps is known as 'philately'.

The most valuable stamp is the British Guiana 1c magenta. There's only one, and it sold for 9.48 million US dollars in 2014.

OTHER CURRENCY SYMBOLS

RUPEE (INDIA)

YUAN (CHINA)

NAIRA (NIGERIA)

COLÓN (COSTA RICA)

WON (KOREA)

It's possible to hammer a piece of gold the size of a grain of rice into a super-thin sheet almost 15 times the size of this page.

Around **40%** of the world's gold was mined from the Witwatersrand rocks in South Africa. This country's currency, the rand, is named after them.

Gases in the air make silver turn black. This is known as tarnishing.

SILVER VARNISH
In museums, silver objects are varnished, so they always look shiny.

Artists Vincent van Gogh and Pablo Picasso both painted pictures inspired by African masks.

Coins called 'florins' were used in Europe for hundreds of years. They're named after the Italian city where they were introduced in 1252: Florence.

The Bayeux Tapestry is 70m (230ft) long and shows scenes from the Norman conquest of England in 1066. It isn't actually a tapestry (a piece of cloth woven with pictures), but an embroidery – because the pictures were sewn into a ready-made piece of cloth.

VBI·NVNTII·VVILLELMI·DVCIS·VENERVNT·AD VVIDO

BUILDINGS

In some parts of Asia, builders use bamboo poles as scaffolding.

The Jeddah Light, in Saudi Arabia, is the tallest lighthouse ever built. It's 133m (436ft) tall.

Over 21,600 truckloads of concrete were used in the construction of the Barbican – a group of buildings in London.

Concrete is made by mixing a powder called cement with water, sand and small pieces of stone.

The world's tallest chimney is in Kazakhstan. It's 419.7m (1,377ft) tall and part of the GRES-2 Power Station.

The Leaning Tower of Pisa in Italy leans at an angle of 3.99 degrees, pointing in a south-easterly direction.

Cranes were invented in Ancient Greece, over 2,500 years ago.

In the 18th century, a Scottish earl named Lord Dunmore added a dome shaped like a pineapple to his summerhouse.

Hong Kong has over 315 skyscrapers – more than any other city in the world.

The wedge-shaped stones in an arch are known as 'voussoirs'.

The Eiffel Tower, in Paris, is made up of around 18,000 metal pieces.

Have you ever seen an arch that's made of two S-shaped curves? It's called an ogee (say oh-jee).

SPACE

THE SUN
is a star at the heart of the **SOLAR SYSTEM**. There are eight planets moving around it whose names are also shown in **CAPITAL** letters.

Space begins 100km (62 miles) above the Earth's surface.

British astronomer Fred Hoyle pointed out that space is, "only an hour's drive away if your car could go straight upwards."

EARTH

VENUS

The Moon

Venus is the hottest of the eight planets.

Water covers over 70% of the Earth's surface.

MARS

Twelve astronauts have walked on the Moon. No one has been there since Eugene Cernan in 1972.

URANUS

A volcano on Mars called Olympus Mons is over two and half times higher than Earth's highest mountain, Everest.

There could be as many as 300 sextillion stars in the Universe. That's

300,000,000,000,000,000,000,000.

'Type O' stars glow blue. They're the hottest type of stars.

William Herschel identified Uranus in 1781. He was a composer before he became an astronomer.

NEPTUNE

Wild winds on Neptune blow at speeds of up to 2,400km/h (1,500mph) – almost twice the speed of sound.

Temperatures on Mercury can plummet 600°C (1,100°F) from day to night.

MERCURY

JUPITER

There's a storm raging on Jupiter known as the 'Great Red Spot'. It's more than twice the size of Earth.

The first animals born in space were Japanese quail chicks. They hatched on March 22, 1990.

Around two million chunks of rock, known as asteroids, make up the Asteroid Belt between Mars and Jupiter.

It's silent in space. This is because there's nothing at all for sounds to move through.

Saturn has over 60 moons. One of them, Enceladus, is covered in ice which makes it the most reflective object in the Solar System.

SATURN

No spacecraft has made it further from Earth than *Voyager 1*. It was launched in 1977 and is still hurtling through space today.

One vast cloud of space dust, or 'nebula', is the shape of a human hand. Its official name is B1509.

Planets outside the Solar System are called exoplanets. The closest exoplanet is Proxima b.

In 2007, US astronaut Sunita Williams became the first person to run a marathon in space. She ran the 42.195km (26 miles, 385 yards) on a treadmill.

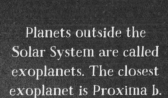

Alexey Leonov went on the first spacewalk outside a spacecraft on March 18, 1965.

RECORD BREAKERS

The oldest known 'and' symbol, or ampersand, was written on a wall in the Roman town of Pompeii more than 1,900 years ago.

Japan has the shortest national anthem. It's just four lines long.

More than 100 MILLION passengers use Hartsfield-Jackson Atlanta International Airport, in the US, each year, making it the world's busiest airport.

Dwarf seahorses are the slowest fish. At their top speed they would take more than 30 hours to swim one length of an Olympic swimming pool.

Actual size

The Library of Congress in Washington DC is the largest library in the world. Its books fill 1,349km (838 miles) of shelves.

The best-selling single of all time is *White Christmas*, sung by Bing Crosby.

The oldest school in the world is in the English city of Canterbury. Known as the King's School, it was founded in the year 597.

Ashrita Furman has set over 500 records - more than any other person. One record was for inflating 28 balloons in three minutes with his nose.

In 2016, scientists created the strongest material ever. Called carbyne, it's 40 times stronger than a diamond.

A stretch of Highway 10 in Saudi Arabia has no corners or bends for 261KM (162 MILES). It's the straightest road in the world.

40 X

458M (1503FT) LONG

The longest ship ever built was an oil tanker called the *Seawise Giant*.

It was longer than New York's Empire State Building is tall.

Vantablack – the blackest black material – absorbs so much light that you can't see it with your eyes.

The mammal that can bite the hardest is the hippopotamus.

In 2004, scientists at a British university studied lots of smelly cheeses and declared a French cheese called Vieux Boulogne the smelliest of them all.

The furriest animals on Earth are sea otters.

A laser used in experiments at the University of Texas produces the brightest light on Earth.

The word 'laser' is an acronym because its letters stand for other words: light amplification (by) stimulated emission (of) radiation.

African driver ant queens lay more eggs than any other animal. One queen can lay up to **4 MILLION** eggs in a month.

Peregrine falcons reach top speeds over **322 KM/H (200 MPH)** as they dive through the air. They're the fastest creatures on the planet.

A red pair of socks knitted in Egypt over **1,600** years ago are the oldest surviving socks in the world.

The tallest type of cactus in the world is the Mexican giant cardon.

19.2M (63FT) TALL

At **45** letters long, pneumonoultramicroscopicsilicovolcanoconiosis is the longest word in the *Oxford English Dictionary*. It's a type of disease that affects the lungs.

The deepest hole ever made is in the Kola Peninsula, in Russia. Scientists drilled more than 12.2km (7.6 miles) into the Earth's crust.